Slow Cooker Poultry Cookbook

Delicious No-Fuss Meals for Carnivores

Mona T. Massey

Sommario

Poultry Recipes 7

Mexican Chicken 9

Chicken in Roasted Red Pepper Sauce 12

Turkey and Potatoes with Buffalo Sauce.......................14

Fall-Off-Bone Chicken Drumsticks..............................16

Coconut Chicken with Tomatoes 18

Cherry Tomato and Basil Chicken Casserole 20

Sweet and Smoked Slow Cooked Turkey.......................23

Chicken and Beans Casserole with Chorizo 25

Creamy Turkey Breasts with Mushrooms......................26

Sweet Gingery and Garlicky Chicken Thighs 29

Simple Pressure Cooked Whole Chicken 31

Chicken Bites Snacks with Chili Sauce 32

Hot and Buttery Chicken Wings 35

Tasty Turkey with Campanelle and Tomato Sauce 36

Chicken with Mushrooms and Leeks 38

Hearty and Hot Turkey Soup 40

Green BBQ Chicken Wings 42

Hot and Spicy Shredded Chicken 43

Homemade Cajun Chicken Jambalaya 45

Salsa and Lime Chicken with Rice 47

Homemade Whole Chicken 49

Herbed and Garlicky Chicken Wings 51

Duck and Green Pea Soup 53

Teriyaki Chicken Under Pressure 55

Young Goose for Slow Cooker 57

Homemade Chicken with Dumplings 59

Mexican-styled Slow Cooker Chicken 61

Yellow Rice with Turkey wings 63

Slow Cooker Turkey Wings 65

Chicken Alfredo in Slow Cooker 67

Quick-to-Cook Chicken 69

Slow Cooker Turkey with Dumplings 71

Flavored Chicken in Rustic Italian Style 73

Hot Turkey Meatballs 75

Shredded Turkey in Barbeque Sauce 77

Lemon-Fragrant Chicken 79

Turkey with Indian Spice 82

Gluten-free Chicken Soup 84

Hawaiian Spice Slow Cooker Chicken 86

Chicken Soup with Rice 88

Tunisian-Styled Turkey **90**

Hot Buffalo Chicken Lettuce Envelopes **92**

Chicken with Pear and Asparagus **94**

Sweet Chicken with Parmesan **96**

Cornish Hens with Olives **98**

Slow Cooker Chicken in Thai Sauce **100**

Leftovers Soup with Turkey Meat **103**

Chicken Livers Mix **105**

Slow Cooker Chicken with Italian dressing **107**

Conclusion **109**

Hey there! Welcome to my publication of recipes for the Crock Pot.

My recipes are simply as well tasty to maintain to myself. As well as it's the only cookbook you'll require to make the most tasty Crockery Pot recipes you have actually ever tasted!

If there's one cooking area device I can not live without, it's my Crockery Pot. This gizmo has actually altered my life completely in the kitchen! Gone are the days when I invested hrs every week, prepping and then cooking meals. Therefore lot of times those meals were tasteless, with leftovers that nobody intended to consume.

Then along came my Crock Pot Pressure Cooker ... and currently I make savory meals on a daily basis.

One of the greatest attractive features of the Crock Pot is that it makes fresh and rapid homey dishes in no time. Whether you're vegetarian or love your meat and also hen, my publication has the most effective recipes for making incredible, healthier meals. As well as see to it you make a luxurious rip off dish on those days when you're not counting calories and also fat! Those are the best recipes of all. In this publication, I share my favorite.

Mexican Chicken

Ready in about: 30 minutes | Serves: 6 | Per serving:
Calories 342; Carbs 11g; Fat 14g; Protein 38g

INGREDIENTS

1 Red Bell Pepper, diced

1 Green Bell Pepper, diced

1 Jalapeno, diced

2 pounds Chicken Breasts

10 ounces canned diced Tomatoes, undrained

1 Red Onion, diced

½ tsp Cumin

¾ tsp Chili Powder

¼ tsp Pepper

Juice of 1 Lime

½ cup Chicken Broth

1 tbsp Olive Oil

DIRECTIONS

Heat oil on SAUTÉ mode at High. When sizzling, add the onion and bell peppers and cook for about 3-4 minutes, until soft.

Add the remaining ingredients and give it a good stir to combine. Seal the lid, press POULTRY set for 15 minutes at High. After it beeps, release the pressure quickly.

Shred the chicken inside the pot with two forks, then stir to combine it with the juices. Serve and enjoy!

Chicken in Roasted Red Pepper Sauce

Ready in about: 25 minutes | Serves: 6 | Per serving: Calories 207; Carbs 5g; Fat 7g; Protein 32g

INGREDIENTS

1 ½ pounds Chicken Breasts, cubed

1 Onion, diced

4 Garlic Cloves

12 ounces Roasted Red Peppers

2 tsp Adobo Sauce

½ cup Beef Broth

1 tbsp Apple Cider Vinegar

1 tsp Cumin

Juice of ½ Lemon

3 tbsp chopped Cilantro

1 tbsp Olive Oil

Salt and Pepper, to taste

DIRECTIONS

Place garlic, red pepper, adobo sauce, lemon juice, vinegar, cilantro, and some salt and pepper, in a food processor. Process until the mixture becomes smooth. Set your pressure cooker to SAUTÉ at High and heat the oil.

Add the onion and cook for 2 minutes. Add the chicken cubes and cook until they are no longer pink. Pour sauce and broth over. Seal the lid, press BEANS/CHILI button, and set the timer to 8 minutes at High pressure.

After you hear the beeping sound, do a quick pressure release. Serve and enjoy!

Turkey and Potatoes with Buffalo Sauce

Ready in about: 30 minutes | Serves: 4 | Per serving: Calories 377; Carbs 32g; Fat 9g; Protein 14g

INGREDIENTS

3 tbsp Olive Oil

4 tbsp Buffalo Sauce

1 pound Sweet Potatoes, cut into cubes

1 ½ pounds Turkey Breast, cut into pieces

½ tsp Garlic Powder

1 Onion, diced

½ cup Water

DIRECTIONS

Heat 1 tbsp of olive oil on SAUTÉ mode at High. Stir-fry onion in hot oil for about 3 minutes. Stir in the remaining ingredients.

Seal the lid, set to MEAT/STEW mode for 20 minutes at High pressure. When cooking is over, do a quick pressure release, by turning the valve to "open" position.

Fall-Off-Bone Chicken Drumsticks

Ready in about: 45 minutes | Serves: 3 | Per serving: Calories 454; Carbs 7g; Fat 27g; Protein 43g

INGREDIENTS

1 tbsp Olive Oil

6 Skinless Chicken Drumsticks

4 Garlic Cloves, smashed

½ Red Bell Pepper, diced

½ Onion, diced

2 tbsp Tomato Paste

2 cups Water

DIRECTIONS

Warm olive oil, and sauté onion and bell pepper, for about 4 minutes, on SAUTÉ at High. Add garlic and cook until golden, for a minute.

Combine the paste with water and pour into the cooker. Arrange the drumsticks inside. Seal the lid, set to POULTRY mode for 20 minutes at High pressure. When it beeps, do a quick pressure release. Serve immediately.

Coconut Chicken with Tomatoes

Ready in about: 25 minutes | Serves: 4 | Per serving: Calories 278; Carbs 28g; Fat 8g; Protein 19g

INGREDIENTS

1 ½ pounds Chicken Thighs

1 ½ cups chopped Tomatoes

1 Onion, chopped

1 ½ tbsp Butter

2 cups Coconut Milk

½ cup chopped Almonds

2 tsp Paprika

1 tsp Garam Masala

2 tbsp Cilantro, chopped

1 tsp Turmeric

1 tsp Cayenne Powder

1 tsp Ginger Powder

1 ¼ tsp Garlic Powder

Salt and Pepper, to taste

DIRECTIONS

Melt butter on SAUTÉ at High. Add the onions and sauté until translucent, for about 3 minutes. Add all spices, and cook for an additional minute, until fragrant. Stir in the tomatoes and coconut milk.

Place the chicken thighs inside and seal the lid. Cook on BEANS/CHILI on High pressure for 13 minutes. When it goes off, do a quick pressure release. Serve topped with chopped almonds and cilantro.

Cherry Tomato and Basil Chicken Casserole

Ready in about: 30 minutes | Serves: 4 | Per serving:
Calories 337; Carbs 12g; Fat 21g; Protein 27g

INGREDIENTS

8 small Chicken Thighs

½ cup Green Olives

1 pound Cherry Tomatoes

1 cup Water

A handful of Fresh Basil Leaves

1 ½ tsp Garlic, minced

1 tsp dried Oregano

1 tbsp Olive Oil

DIRECTIONS

Season chicken with salt and pepper. Melt butter on SAUTÉ at High, and brown the chicken for about 2 minutes per side. Place tomatoes in a plastic bag and smash with a meat pounder.

Remove the chicken to a plate.

Combine tomatoes, garlic, water, and oregano in the pressure cooker. Top with the chicken and seal the lid. Cook on POULTRY at High for 15 minutes. When ready, do a quick pressure release. Stir in the basil and olives.

Sweet and Smoked Slow Cooked Turkey

Ready in about: 4 hours 15 minutes | Serves: 4 | Per serving: Calories 513; Carbs 15 g; Fat 42g; Protein 65g

INGREDIENTS

1.5 pounds Turkey Breast

2 tsp Smoked Paprika

1 tsp Liquid Smoke

1 tbsp Mustard

3 tbsp Honey

2 Garlic Cloves, minced

4 tbsp Olive Oil

1 cup Chicken Broth

DIRECTIONS

Brush the turkey breast with olive oil and brown it on all sides, for 3-4 minutes, on SAUTÉ at High. Pour the chicken broth and all remaining ingredients in a bowl. Stir to combine.

Pour the mixture over the meat. Seal the lid, set on SLOW COOK mode for 4 hours. Do a quick pressure release.

Chicken and Beans Casserole with Chorizo

Ready in about: 35 minutes | Serves: 5 | Per serving: Calories 587; Carbs 52g; Fat 29g; Protein 29g

INGREDIENTS

1 tsp Garlic, minced

1 cup Onions, chopped

1 pound Chorizo Sausage, cut into pieces

4 Chicken Thighs, boneless, skinless

3 tbsp Olive Oil

2 cups Chicken Stock

11 ounces Asparagus, quartered

1 tsp Paprika

½ tsp ground Black Pepper

1 tsp Salt

2 Jalapeno Peppers, stemmed, cored, and chopped

26 oz canned whole Tomatoes, roughly chopped

1 ½ cups Kidney Beans

DIRECTIONS

On SAUTÉ, heat the oil and brown the sausage, for about 5 minutes per side. Transfer to a large bowl. In the same oil, add the thighs and brown them for 5 minutes. Remove to the same bowl as the sausage.

In the cooker, stir in onions and peppers. Cook for 3 minutes. Add in garlic and cook for 1 minute. Stir in the tomatoes, beans, stock, asparagus, paprika, salt, and black pepper.

Return the reserved sausage and thighs to the cooker. Stir well. Seal the lid and cook for 10 minutes on BEANS/CHILI mode at High Pressure. When ready, do a quick release and serve hot.

Creamy Turkey Breasts with Mushrooms

Ready in about: 35 minutes | Serves: 4 | Per serving: Calories 192; Carbs 5g; Fat 12g; Protein 15g

INGREDIENTS

20 ounces Turkey Breasts, boneless and skinless

6 ounces White Button Mushrooms, sliced

3 tbsp Shallots, chopped

½ tsp dried Thyme

¼ cup dry White Wine

cup Chicken Stock

1 Garlic Clove, minced

2 tbsp Olive Oil

3 tbsp Heavy Cream

1 ½ tbsp Cornstarch

Salt and Pepper, to taste

DIRECTIONS

Warm half of the olive oil on SAUTÉ mode at High. Meanwhile, tie turkey breast with a kitchen string horizontally, leaving approximately 2 inches apart. Season the meat with salt and pepper. Add the turkey to the pressure cooker and cook for about 3 minutes on each side. Transfer to a plate. Heat the remaining oil and cook shallots, thyme, garlic, and mushrooms until soft.

Add white wine and scrape up the brown bits from the bottom. When the alcohol evaporates, return the turkey to the pressure cooker. Seal the lid, and cook on MEAT/STEW for 25 minutes at High.

Meanwhile, combine heavy cream and cornstarch in a small bowl. Do a quick pressure release. Open the lid and stir in the mixture. Bring the sauce to a boil, then turn the cooker off. Slice the turkey in half and serve topped with the creamy mushroom sauce.

Sweet Gingery and Garlicky Chicken Thighs

Ready in about: 25 minutes | Serves: 4 | Per serving: Calories 561; Carbs 61g; Fat 21g; Protein 54g

INGREDIENTS

2 pounds Chicken Thighs

½ cup Honey

3 tsp grated Ginger

2 tbsp Garlic, minced

5 tbsp Brown Sugar

2 cups Chicken Broth

½ cup plus 2 tbsp Soy Sauce

½ cup plus 2 tbsp Hoisin Sauce

4 tbsp Sriracha

2 tbsp Sesame Oil

DIRECTIONS

Lay the chicken at the bottom. Mix the remaining ingredients in a bowl. Pour the mixture over the chicken.

Seal the lid, select POULTRY and set the time to 20 minutes at High. Do a quick pressure release.

Simple Pressure Cooked Whole Chicken

Ready in about: 40 minutes | Serves: 4 | Per serving: Calories 376; Carbs 0g; Fat 30g; Protein 25g

INGREDIENTS

1 2-pound Whole Chicken

2 tbsp Olive Oil

1 ½ cups Water

Salt and Pepper, to taste

DIRECTIONS

Season chicken all over with salt and pepper. Heat the oil on SAUTÉ at High, and cook the chicken until browned on all sides. Set aside and wipe clean the cooker. Insert a rack in your pressure cooker and pour the water in.

Lower the chicken onto the rack. Seal the lid. Choose POULTRY setting and adjust the time to 25 minutes at High pressure. Once the cooking is over, do a quick pressure release, by turning the valve to "open" position.

Chicken Bites Snacks with Chili Sauce

Ready in about: 25 minutes | Serves: 6 | Per serving:
Calories 405; Carbs 18g; Fat 19g; Protein 31g

INGREDIENTS

1 ½ pounds Chicken, cut up, with bones

¼ cup Tomato Sauce

Kosher Salt and Black Pepper to taste

2 tsp dry Basil

¼ cup raw Honey

1 ½ cups Water

FOR CHILI SAUCE:

2 spicy Chili Peppers, halved

½ cup loosely packed Parsley, finely chopped

1 tsp Sugar

1 clove Garlic, chopped

2 tbsp Lime juice

¼ cup Olive Oil

DIRECTIONS

Put a steamer basket in the cooker's pot and pour the water in. Place the meat in the basket, and press BEANS/CHILI button. Seal the lid and cook for 20 minutes at High Pressure.

Meanwhile, prepare the sauce by mixing all the sauce ingredients in a food processor. Blend until the pepper is chopped and all the ingredients are mixed well. Release the pressure quickly. To serve, place the meat in serving bowl and top with the sauce.

Hot and Buttery Chicken Wings

Ready in about: 20 minutes | Serves: 16 | Per serving: Calories 50; Carbs 1g; Fat 2g; Protein 7g

INGREDIENTS

16 Chicken Wings

1 cup Hot Sauce

1 cup Water

2 tbsp Butter

DIRECTIONS

Add in all ingredients, and seal the lid. Cook on MEAT/STEW for 15 minutes at High. When ready, press CANCEL and release the pressure naturally, for 10 minutes.

Tasty Turkey with Campanelle and Tomato Sauce

Ready in about: 20 minutes | Serves: 4 | Per serving: Calories 588; Carbs 71g; Fat 11g; Protein 60g

INGREDIENTS

3 cups Tomato Sauce

½ tsp Salt

½ tbsp Marjoram

1 tsp dried Thyme

½ tbsp fresh Basil, chopped

¼ tsp ground Black Pepper, or more to taste

1 ½ pounds Turkey Breasts, chopped

1 tsp Garlic, minced

1 ½ cup spring Onions, chopped

1 package dry Campanelle Pasta

2 tbsp Olive Oil

½ cup Grana Padano cheese, grated

DIRECTIONS

Select SAUTÉ at High and heat the oil in the cooker. Place the turkey, spring onions and garlic. Cook until cooked, about 6-7 minutes. Add the remaining ingredients, except the cheese.

Seal the lid and press BEANS/CHILI button. Cook for 5 minutes at High Pressure. Once cooking has completed, quick release the pressure. To serve, top with freshly grated Grana Padano cheese.

Chicken with Mushrooms and Leeks

Ready in about: 25 minutes | Serves: 6 | Per serving: Calories 321; Carbs 31g; Fat 18g; Protein 39g

INGREDIENTS

2 pounds Chicken Breasts, cubed

4 tbsp Butter

1 ¼ pounds Mushrooms, sliced

½ cup Chicken Broth

2 tbsp Cornstarch

½ cup Milk

¼ tsp Black Pepper

2 Leeks, sliced

¼ tsp Garlic Powder

DIRECTIONS

Melt butter on SAUTÉ mode at High. Place chicken cubes inside and cook until they are no longer pink, and become slightly golden. Transfer the chicken pieces to a plate.

Add the leeks and sliced mushrooms to the pot and cook for about 3 minutes. Return the chicken to the pressure cooker, season with pepper and garlic powder, and pour in broth.

Give the mixture a good stir to combine everything well, then seal the lid. Set on BEANS/CHILI mode, for 8 minutes at High pressure. When it goes off, release the pressure quickly.

In a bowl, whisk together the milk and cornstarch. Pour the mixture over the chicken and set the pressure cooker to SAUTÉ at High. Cook until the sauce thickens.

Hearty and Hot Turkey Soup

**Ready in about: 40 minutes | Serves: 6 | Per serving:
Calories 398; Carbs 40g; Fat 11g; Protein 51g**

INGREDIENTS

1 ½ pounds Turkey thighs, boneless, skinless and diced

1 cup Carrots, trimmed and diced

2 (8 oz) cans White Beans

2 Tomatoes, chopped

1 potato, chopped

1 cup Green Onions, chopped

2 Cloves Garlic, minced

6 cups Vegetable Stock

¼ tsp ground Black Pepper

¼ tsp Salt

½ tsp Cayenne Pepper

½ cup Celery head, peeled and chopped

DIRECTIONS

Place all ingredients, except the beans, into the pressure cooker, and select SOUP mode. Seal the lid and cook for 20 minutes at High Pressure. Release the pressure quickly.

Remove the lid and stir in the beans. Cover the cooker and let it stand for 10 minutes before serving.

Green BBQ Chicken Wings

Ready in about: 20 minutes | Serves: 4 | Per serving: Calories 311; Carbs 1g; Fat 10g; Protein 51g

INGREDIENTS

2 pounds Chicken Wings

5 tbsp Butter

1 cup Barbeque Sauce

5 Green Onions, minced

DIRECTIONS

Add the butter, ¾ parts of the sauce and chicken in the pressure cooker. Select POULTRY, seal the lid and cook for 15 minutes at High.

Do a quick release. Garnish wings with onions and top with the remaining sauce.

Hot and Spicy Shredded Chicken

Ready in about: 1 hour | Serves: 4 | Per serving: Calories 307; Carbs 12g; Fat 10g; Protein 38g

INGREDIENTS

1 ½ pounds boneless and skinless Chicken Breasts

2 cups diced Tomatoes

½ tsp Oregano

2 Green Chilies, seeded and chopped

½ tsp Paprika

2 tbsp Coconut Sugar

½ cup Salsa

1 tsp Cumin

2 tbsp Olive Oil

DIRECTIONS

In a small mixing dish, combine the oil with all spices. Rub the chicken breast with the spicy marinade. Lay the meat into your pressure cooker. Add the tomatoes. Seal the lid, and cook for 20 minutes on POULTRY at High.

Once ready, do a quick pressure release. Remove chicken to a cutting board; shred it. Return the shredded chicken to the cooker. Set to SAUTÉ at High, and let simmer for about 15 minutes.

Homemade Cajun Chicken Jambalaya

Ready in about: 30 minutes | Serves: 6 | Per serving: Calories 299; Carbs 31g; Fat 8g; Protein 41g

INGREDIENTS

1 ½ pounds, Chicken Breast, skinless

3 cups Chicken Stock

1 tbsp Garlic, minced

1 tsp Cajun Seasoning

1 Celery stalk, diced

1 ½ cups chopped Leeks, white part

1 ½ cups dry White Rice

2 tbsp Tomato Paste

DIRECTIONS

Select SAUTÉ at High and brown the chicken for 5 minutes. Add the garlic and celery, and fry for 2 minutes until fragrant. Deglaze with broth. Add the remaining ingredients to the cooker. Seal the lid.

Select POULTRY, and cook for 15 minutes at High. Do a quick pressure release and serve

Salsa and Lime Chicken with Rice

Ready in about: 35 minutes | Serves: 4 | Per serving: Calories 403; Carbs 44g; Fat 16g; Protein 19g

INGREDIENTS

¼ cup Lime Juice

3 tbsp Olive Oil

½ cup Salsa

2 Frozen Chicken Breasts, boneless and skinless

½ tsp Garlic Powder

1 cup Rice

1 cup Water

½ tsp Pepper

½ cup Mexican Cheese Blend

½ cup Tomato Sauce

DIRECTIONS

Lay the chicken into the pressure cooker. Pour lime juice, salt, garlic powder, olive oil, tomato sauce, and pepper, over the chicken. Seal the lid, and cook for 15 minutes on MEAT/STEW mode at High.

When ready, do a quick pressure release. Remove the chicken to a plate. Add in rice, cooking juices and water the total liquid in the pressure cooker should be about 2 cups.

Seal the lid and adjust the time to 10 minutes on BEANS/CHILI at High pressure. Do a quick pressure release and serve with cooked rice.

Homemade Whole Chicken

Ready in about: 40 minutes | Serves: 6 | Per serving:
Calories 207; Carbs 1g; Fat 8g; Protein 29g

INGREDIENTS

3 - pound Whole Chicken

1 cup Chicken Broth

1 ½ tbsp Olive Oil

1 tsp Paprika

¾ tsp Garlic Powder

¼ tsp Onion Powder

DIRECTIONS

Rinse chicken under cold water, remove the giblets, and pat it dry with some paper towels. In a small bowl, combine the oil and spices. Rub the chicken well with the mixture. Set your pressure cooker to SAUTÉ at High. Add the chicken and sear on all sides until golden.

Pour the chicken broth around the chicken not over it), and seal the lid. Cook on BEANS/CHILI, for 25 minutes at High. Do a quick pressure release. Transfer the chicken to a platter and let sit for 10 minutes before carving.

Herbed and Garlicky Chicken Wings

Ready in about: 25 minutes | Serves: 4 | Per serving:
Calories 177; Carbs 1g; Fat 10g; Protein 19g

INGREDIENTS

12 Chicken Wings

½ cup Chicken Broth

1 tbsp Basil

1 tbsp Oregano

½ tbsp Tarragon

1 tbsp Garlic, minced

2 tbsp Olive Oil

¼ tsp Pepper

1 cup Water

DIRECTIONS

Pour the water in the pressure cooker and lower the rack. Place all ingredients in a bowl and mix with your hands to combine well. Cover the bowl and let the wings sit for 15 minutes.

Arrange on the rack and seal the lid. Select BEANS/CHILI, and set the timer to 10 minutes at High pressure. When done, do a quick pressure release. Serve drizzled with the cooking liquid and enjoy!

Duck and Green Pea Soup

Ready in about: 30 minutes | Serves: 6 | Per serving: Calories 191; Carbs 14g; Fat 5g; Protein 21g

INGREDIENTS

1 cup Carrots, diced

4 cups Chicken Stock

1 pound Duck Breasts, chopped

20 ounces diced canned Tomatoes

1 cup Celery, chopped

18 ounces Green Peas

1 cup Onions, diced

2 Garlic Cloves, minced

1 tsp dried Marjoram

½ tsp Pepper

½ tsp Salt

DIRECTIONS

Place all ingredients, except the peas, in your pressure cooker. Stir well to combine and seal the lid. Select SOUP mode and set the cooking time to 20 minutes at High.

After the beep, do a quick pressure release. Stir in the peas. Seal the lid again but do NOT turn the pressure cooker on. Let blanch for about 7 minutes. Ladle into serving bowls.

Teriyaki Chicken Under Pressure

Ready in about: 25 minutes | Serves: 8 | Per serving:
Calories 352; Carbs 31g; Fat 11g; Protein 31g

INGREDIENTS

1 cup Chicken Broth

¾ cup Brown Sugar

2 tbsp ground Ginger

1 tsp Pepper

3 pounds Boneless and Skinless Chicken Thighs

¼ cup Apple Cider Vinegar

¾ cup low-sodium Soy Sauce

20 ounces canned Pineapple, crushed

2 tbsp Garlic Powder

DIRECTIONS

Stir all of the ingredients, except for the chicken. Add the chicken meat and turn to coat. Seal the lid, press POULTRY and cook for 20 minutes at High. Do a quick pressure release, by turning the valve to "open" position.

Young Goose for Slow Cooker

The mild taste of wild goose!

Prep time: 21 minutes Cooking time: 6 hours Servings: 6

INGREDIENTS:

3 tbsp fresh rosemary

Chopped celery

Cream of mushroom soup

Fresh sage

2 goose

Cream of celery soup

Fresh thyme

Cream of chicken soup

1 cup mushrooms

1 pack baby carrots

DIRECTIONS:

Finely mince fresh thyme, rosemary, and sage leaves. Chop celery and baby carrots.

In a wide bowl, mix cream of celery, carrots, cream of chicken soup. Celery, cream of mushroom soup, sage, thyme, mushrooms and rosemary.

Cut goose into pieces and place into Slow Cooker. Pour the cream mixture over the meat.

Set to HIGH and cook for 8 hours until tender.

Nutrition: Calories: 998 Fat: 56g Carbohydrates: 17g Protein: 91g

Homemade Chicken with Dumplings

Try this freshly cooked chicken with your family!

Prep time: 21 minutes Cooking time: 6 hours Servings: 6

INGREDIENTS:

1 cup water

4 cans chicken broth

4 carrots

Salt

2 tbsp flour

4 baking potatoes

2 cups baking mix

2 cups chopped broccoli

Black pepper

4 tbsp milk

DIRECTIONS:

Right in Slow Cooker, mix potatoes, chicken meat, broccoli and carrots.

In a separate bowl, mix water and flour until it appears to be paste-like. Season with pepper and salt to taste.

Pour in over the Slow Cooker ingredients and stir well. Cover and cook for 5 hours on LOW mode.

In small bowl, combine baking mix and milk. Carefully add to Slow Cooker, using a teaspoon. Cook for another hour.

**Nutrition: Calories: 649 Fat: 22g Carbohydrates: 62g
Protein: 47g**

Mexican-styled Slow Cooker Chicken

Add this to your tacos and salads, or just serve with pasta or rice!

Prep time: 11 minutes Cooking time: 4 hours Servings: 4

INGREDIENTS:

Half cup tomato salsa

Half cup tomato preserves

Half cup chipotle salsa

One chicken

DIRECTIONS:

In a bowl, mix pineapple preserves, chipotle salsa and tomato salsa. If needed, remove skin and bones from the chicken meat.

Place chicken into Slow Cooker and pour over with the sauce. Toss meat to cover evenly. Cook for 3 hours on LOW mode.

Remove chicken meat from Slow Cooker and finely shred with two forks. Return to Slow Cooker and prepare for 1 more hour.

**Nutrition: Calories: 238 Fat: 2g Carbohydrates: 31g
Protein: 23g**

Yellow Rice with Turkey wings

Quick and easy for working days!

Prep time: 21 minutes Cooking time: 6 hours Servings: 6

INGREDIENTS:

1 tsp seasoned salt

3 turkey wings

1 tsp garlic powder

Ground black pepper

Water to cover

Cream of mushroom soup

1 pack saffron rice

DIRECTIONS:

Clean the turkey wings and transfer to Slow Cooker.

In a bowl, mix garlic powder, salt, cream of mushroom soup, black pepper. Season the wings with this mixture.

Pour in water into Slow Cooker – just enough to cover the wings. Stir everything well and cover. Cook for 8 hours on LOW mode.

When it is time, stir the rice into Slow Cooker and prepare for 20 minutes more.

Nutrition: Calories: 272 Fat: 5g Carbohydrates: 39g Protein: 17g

Slow Cooker Turkey Wings

You can try it with your favorite sauce and side dishes!

Prep time: 11 minutes Cooking time: 7 hours Servings: 12

INGREDIENTS:

Salt

Ground black pepper

6 turkey legs

3 tsp poultry seasoning

DIRECTIONS:

Wash the turkey legs with running water and remove excess liquid.

Rub each turkey leg with one teaspoon of poultry seasoning. Add salt and black pepper. Cut aluminum foil into leg-fitting parts and wrap each turkey leg with a foil.

Place the wrapped legs into Slow Cooker. Add no water or other liquids. Cook on LOW for 8 hours. Check the tenderness before serving.

Nutrition: Calories: 217 Fat: 7g Carbohydrates: 1g Protein: 36g

Chicken Alfredo in Slow Cooker

Easy with Alfredo sauce and Swiss cheese!

Prep time: 16 minutes Cooking time: 4 hours Servings: 6

INGREDIENTS:

Black pepper

3 tbsp grated Parmesan cheese

4 chicken breast halves

Salt

4 slices Swiss cheese

Garlic powder

DIRECTIONS:

Wash your chicken breasts with running water. Remove the bones and skin. Cut chicken meat into small cubes.

Right in Slow Cooker, combine chicken cubes and Alfredo sauce. Toss to cover. Cook under lid on LOW mode, approximately for two hours.

Add both cheeses and cook for another 30 minutes.

Just before serving, season with salt, garlic powder and black pepper to taste.

Nutrition: Calories: 610 Fat: 50g Carbohydrates: 9g Protein: 31g

Quick-to-Cook Chicken

It will wait for you to come home!

Prep time: 16 minutes Cooking time: 8 hours Servings: 6

INGREDIENTS:

Half cup sour cream

4 chicken breast halves

Cream of celery

Cream of chicken soup

DIRECTIONS:

Discard the skin and bones from the chicken. Wash and drain.

Grease your Slow Cooker with melted butter or olive oil. If you prefer cooking spray, use it. Transfer cleared chicken into Slow Cooker.

In a bowl, whisk both creams. Mix well until smooth. Pour the chicken meat with cream mixture.

Cover with the lid and prepare for 8 hours on LOW mode. Just before serving, add the sour cream.

To serve, transfer cooked chicken onto a large bowl. Garnish with chopped green onion or other vegetables or berries. Serve hot.

Nutrition: Calories: 304 Fat: 16g Carbohydrates: 12g Protein: 27g

Slow Cooker Turkey with Dumplings

Creamy and hot, perfect choice for a cold day!

Prep time: 9 minutes Cooking time: 4 hours Servings: 4

INGREDIENTS:

3 medium carrots

1 cans cream of chicken soup

Garlic powder

1 can chicken broth

Half onion

Buttermilk biscuit dough

5 large potatoes

2 tbsp butter

Cooked turkey

Poultry seasoning

DIRECTIONS:

Cook the turkey before start.

Chop the potatoes, onion and carrots.

In a bowl, mix butter, onion, potatoes, turkey, chicken broth and cream of chicken soup. Season with garlic powder.

Transfer into Slow Cooker and pour in water to cover. Cook on HIGH mode for 3 hours, stirring occasionally. Place the biscuits over turkey and cook for 1 more hour

Nutrition: Calories: 449 Fat: 22g Carbohydrates: 38g Protein: 23g

Flavored Chicken in Rustic Italian Style

Perfect with veggies and Italian seasoning!

Prep time: 22 minutes Cooking time: 5 hours Servings: 6

INGREDIENTS:

3 cups penne pasta

Red bell pepper

Chicken thighs

Canned tomatoes

Salt

Canned crushed tomatoes

Black pepper

Fresh mushrooms

2 carrots

4 garlic cloves

DIRECTIONS:

Grease Slow Cooker with oil or spray with anti-stick cooking spray. Transfer chicken to Slow Cooker.

Chop carrots into 1-inch slices, slice bell peppers and mushrooms. Mice garlic.

Add the vegetables and add canned tomatoes, salt/pepper and season with two tablespoons of Italian seasoning.

Cover and cook on LOW for 8 hours.

To serve, use 3 cups penne pasta or fresh parsley.

Nutrition: Calories: 441 Fat: 16g Carbohydrates: 41g Protein: 31g

Hot Turkey Meatballs

Perfectly to serve with vegetables!

Prep time: 17 minutes Cooking time: 3 hours Servings: 4

INGREDIENTS:

Water

Dry onion soup mix (2 envelopes)

2 Chicken eggs

Beef flavored rice

Fresh turkey meat

DIRECTIONS:

Fill your Slow Cooker with water and onion soup mix (there should be enough liquid to fill crockpot halfway).

Turn on Slow Cooker to high and leave until the liquid boils.

Meanwhile, make meatballs. In a bowl, combine rice with turkey and flavoring mix. Add beaten chicken eggs and mix together.

Form 2-inch meatballs and fry them to brown on large skillet with oil.

When soup is boiling. Transfer meatballs to Slow Cooker and prepare 9 hours on LOW temperature mode.

Nutrition: Calories: 567 Fat: 22g Carbohydrates: 42g Protein: 47g

Shredded Turkey in Barbeque Sauce

Full of protein and healthy meal!

Prep time: 13 minutes Cooking time: 10 hours Servings: 8

INGREDIENTS:

1 tsp ground cumin

8 potato rolls

2 cans baked beans

1 medium onion

1 tbsp yellow mustard

2 bone-in turkey thighs

salt

DIRECTIONS:

Finely chop onion.

Grease your Slow Cooker with melted plain butter.

Right in Slow Cooker pot, combine onion, baked beans, barbeque sauce, cumin, yellow mustard and salt.

Carefully place the turkey thighs into the mixture.

Set Slow Cooker to LOW temperature and cook for 11 hours.

Remove turkey and discard bones. Shred and place back to Slow Cooker. Serve the turkey placed over potato rolls.

Nutrition: Calories: 385 Fat: 6g Carbohydrates: 59g Protein: 26g

Lemon-Fragrant Chicken

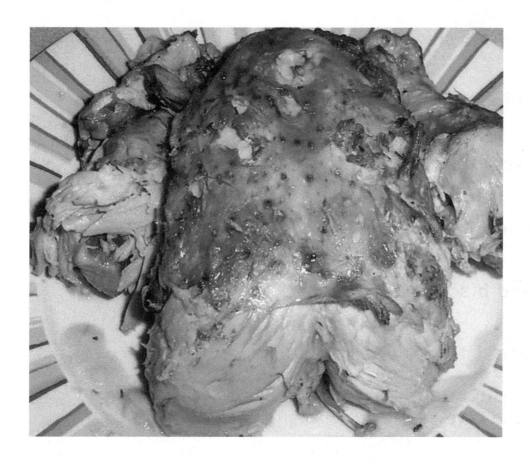

Easy and great to taste!

Prep time: 22 minutes Cooking time: 9 hours Servings: 6

INGREDIENTS:

1 medium onion

1 cup hot water

Salt

One stalk celery

One whole chicken

One big apple

Half tsp dried rosemary

zest and juice of 1 lemon

ground black pepper

DIRECTIONS:

Peel and core apple. Cut into quarters.

Wash the chicken and dry with a paper towel.

Rub the salt and pepper mix into chickens' skin and place apple and chopped celery into chicken. Place chicken into Slow Cooker and sprinkle with chopped onion, lemon zest and juice, rosemary. Pour in one cup water.

Cover and cook on HIGH for 1 hour. Then, turn to LOW and cook for 7 hours.

**Nutrition: Calories: 309 Fat: 17g Carbohydrates: 7g
Protein: 31g**

Turkey with Indian Spice

Perfect with rice and fresh herbs!

Prep time: 17 minutes Cooking time: 6 hours Servings: 4

INGREDIENTS:

Turkey thigh meat

Canned stewed tomatoes

3 tbsp dried onion flakes

Dried thyme leaves

4 tbsp white wine

Half tsp Italian seasoning

6 cubes chicken bouillon

Garlic powder

Lemon pepper seasoning

DIRECTIONS:

In a bowl, whisk together wine and canned tomatoes.

Pour in the tomato mixture into your Slow Cooker and add onion flakes, bouillon cubes and thyme. Season with garlic powder and Italian seasoning.

Carefully place the turkey into Slow Cooker.

Cover the lid and cook for 10 hours on LOW temperature mode.

Nutrition: Calories: 317 Fat: 7g Carbohydrates: 9g Protein: 51g

Gluten-free Chicken Soup

Easy to cook on a busy day!

Prep time: 13 minutes Cooking time: 8 hours Servings: 9

INGREDIENTS:

Medium onion

1/2 cup water

2 carrots

Gluten-free chicken broth

Salt

Frozen vegetables

4 tbsp. long-grain rice

2 celery stalks

Garlic

Black pepper

Dried basil

tomatoes

Red pepper flakes

DIRECTIONS:

In a bowl, combine diced tomatoes, diced carrots, garlic, celery and onions.

Transfer the vegetable mix into Slow Cooker and season with dried basil, red pepper flakes, salt and pepper.

Carefully place chicken into the mixture. Stir everything well to cover the meat. Cook on LOW temperature mode for 7 hours.

Add rice and frozen vegetable mix. Cook for 1 more hour on HIGH.

Nutrition: Calories: 198 Fat: 6g Carbohydrates: 20g
Protein: 16g

Hawaiian Spice Slow Cooker Chicken

Amazingly tastes with rice!

Prep time: 5 minutes Cooking time: 4 hours Servings: 9

INGREDIENTS:

Chicken breasts

Canned sliced pineapples

1 tsp soy sauce

1 bottle honey bbq sauce

DIRECTIONS:

Carefully grease the bottom and sides of your Slow Cooker with melted butter or spray with anti- stick spray.

Wash and drain chicken breasts, place into Slow Cooker.

In a bowl, mix pineapple slices and barbeque sauce, add soy sauce. Pour in this mixture over chicken breasts into Slow Cooker.

Cover the lid and turn Slow Cooker to HIGH temperature mode. Cook for 5 hours. To serve, garnish chicken with chopped parsley and green onion. Serve while hot.

Nutrition: Calories: 274 Fat: 3g Carbohydrates: 29g Protein: 30g

Chicken Soup with Rice

Your whole family will like this soup!

Prep time: 5 minutes Cooking time: 8 hours Servings: 6

INGREDIENTS:

3 celery sticks

4 tbsp long-grain rice

2 cups frozen mixed vegetables

Half cup water

1 tbsp dried parsley

Lemon seasoning

3 cans chicken broth

Herb seasoning

DIRECTIONS:

Remove bones from chicken breast halves. Cook and dice the meat. In a bowl, combine chopped celery, rice, mixed vegetables.

Season the mixture with lemon and herbal seasoning. Add some salt to taste and transfer to Slow Cooker.

Whisk water and chicken broth; pour over the vegetable and chicken mixture in Slow Cooker. Cover and cook for 8 hours, using LOW temperature mode.

Nutrition: Calories: 277 Fat: 7g Carbohydrates: 27g Protein: 25g

Tunisian-Styled Turkey

Satisfying and tasty dish for any holiday!

Prep time: 11 minutes Cooking time: 4 hours Servings: 6

INGREDIENTS:

2 tbsp flour

1 turkey breast half

Chipotle chili powder

1 tbsp olive oil

Half tsp garlic powder

1 acorn squash

Ground cinnamon

3 large carrots

Coriander

2 red onions

Salt

6 garlic cloves

Ground black pepper

DIRECTIONS:

Mix chipotle and garlic powder, black pepper, cinnamon and salt.

Rub turkey meat with spicy mix and brown in a large skillet (use medium heat). Grease your Slow Cooker with olive oil.

Cover the bottom of Slow Cooker with diced carrots, acorn squash quarters, garlic cloves and red onions.

Place the turkey atop the vegetables. Cook on HIGH mode for 8 hours.

Nutrition: Calories: 455 Fat: 5g Carbohydrates: 19g Protein: 81g

Hot Buffalo Chicken Lettuce Envelopes

So much healthier than traditional Buffalo wings!

Prep time: 11 minutes Cooking time: 6 hours Servings: 10

INGREDIENTS:

2 chicken breasts

1 pack ranch dressing mix

One head Boston lettuce leaves

Cayenne pepper sauce

DIRECTIONS:

Remove skin and bones from the chicken and put the breasts into Slow Cooker.

In a bowl, stir to smooth ranch dressing mix and cayenne pepper. Stir the mixture until it is smooth.

Pour the chicken breasts with the sauce. Make sure that all the chicken surface is covered with the sayce.

Cover and cook during 7 hours (use LOW temperature mode).

Using spotted spoon, place chicken meat over the lettuce leaves and roll.

Nutrition: Calories: 105 Fat: 2g Carbohydrates: 2g Protein: 18g

Chicken with Pear and Asparagus

Unusual seasoning for incredibly tasty dish!

Prep time: 21 minutes Cooking time: 4 hours Servings: 4

INGREDIENTS:

4 cloves garlic

1 tbsp vegetable oil

2 tbsp balsamic vinegar

4 chicken breast halves

3 tbsp apple juice

One onion

Dried rosemary

Black pepper, salt

Grated fresh ginger

Two Bartlett pears

2 tbsp brown sugar

Fresh asparagus

DIRECTIONS:

Core and slice Bartlett pears.

Warm the olive on preheated skillet. Cook chicken meat until it is completely browned. Transfer to Slow Cooker.

Dice the onion and spread it over the chicken. Season with salt and pepper.

Place asparagus and pears into Slow Cooker.

Separately mix balsamic vinegar, sugar, apple juice, sugar, ginger and garlic. Add to Slow Cooker. Cover and cook for 5 hours on LOW mode.

Nutrition: Calories: 309 Fat: 7g Carbohydrates: 33g Protein: 29g

Sweet Chicken with Parmesan

This one will be your favorite!

Prep time: 11 minutes Cooking time: 5 hours Servings: 6

INGREDIENTS:

Black pepper

6 tbsp butter

Salt to taste

Onion soup mix

Cream of mushroom soup

Grated Parmesan

1 cup milk

1 cup rice

6 chicken breasts

DIRECTIONS:

Remove skin and bones off the chicken.

Separately mix milk, onion soup mix, rice and cream of mushroom soup. Slightly grease Slow Cooker, lay chicken meat over the bottom.

Pour the sauce mixture all over it.

In addition, season with pepper/salt.

Finally, cover with grated Parmesan cheese.

Set Slow Cooker to LOW and prepare for 10 hours.

Nutrition: Calories: 493 Fat: 21g Carbohydrates: 37g Protein: 35g

Cornish Hens with Olives

Perfect with wild rice or vegetables!

Prep time: 21 minutes Cooking time: 4 hours Servings: 2

INGREDIENTS:

1 tsp garlic salt

2 Cornish game hens

One large zucchini

Golden mushroom soup

Pimento-stuffed green olives

Baby Portobello mushrooms

DIRECTIONS:

To start, prepare the vegetables: chop zucchini, mushrooms and green olives. Slightly coat the hens with 3 tablespoons of golden mushroom soup.

In a bowl, mix olives, remaining mushroom soup, garlic salt and zucchini. Stuff the hens with this mixture.

Transfer hens into Slow Cooker and pour over with some more mushroom soup (all that remained).

Set your Slow Cooker to HIGH mode and cook for 4 hours.

Nutrition: Calories: 851 Fat: 57g Carbohydrates: 24g Protein: 59g

Slow Cooker Chicken in Thai Sauce

Slightly spiced, this is an awesome dish for any occasion!

Prep time: 23 minutes Cooking time: 5 hours Servings: 6

INGREDIENTS:

Half cup roasted peanuts

6 chicken breast halves

Fresh cilantro

1 large bell pepper

3 green onions

Large onion

Chicken broth

Soy sauce

3 cloves garlic

2 tbsp cornstarch

Salt/pepper

6 tbsp creamy butter cream

1 tbsp ground cumin

Red pepper flakes

DIRECTIONS:

Grease your Slow Cooker with melted butter.

Right in a cooking pot, combine chopped bell pepper, onion and chopped to trips chicken. In a bowl, whisk together red pepper flakes, minced garlic, cumin, pepper/salt. Stir to blend. Cover Slow Cooker with the lid and cook for 5 hours on low mode.

Drain 1 cup liquid from Slow Cooker to whisk lime juice, soy sauce, peanut butter and cornstarch in it. Pour in back to Slow Coker.

Cook on HIGH for 30 minutes more.

To serve, garnish with cilantro, green onions and chopped peanuts.

**Nutrition: Calories: 410 Fat: 26g Carbohydrates: 18g
Protein: 35g**

Leftovers Soup with Turkey Meat

A hearty soup with noodles and turkey for your family!

Prep time: 23 minutes Cooking time: 10 hours Servings: 8

INGREDIENTS:

2 cups penne pasts

Chicken broth

Small onion

Cream of mushroom soup

One turkey carcass

2 bay leaves

3 cup cooked turkey

Chopped celery

3 celery steaks

One quartered onion

2 medium carrots

DIRECTIONS:

Place the turkey carcass into your Slow Cooker.

Place quartered onion, halved celery and carrots and bay leaves into Slow Cooker too. Cover and cook for approximately 4 hours. Carefully remove solids from Slow Cooker. Add chopped vegetables and cook for 3 hours on LOW regime.

Add penne paste and leave to prepare for additional 2 hours.

In the end of time, mix in mushroom cream and turkey meat. Cook for 30 minutes.

Nutrition: Calories: 1876 Fat: 140g Carbohydrates: 54g Protein: 87g

Chicken Livers Mix

Perfect with noodles and rice!

Prep time: 34 minutes Cooking time: 6-7 hours Servings: 4

INGREDIENTS:

3 green onions

1 tsp salt

Dry white wine

3 slices bacon

Black pepper

One cup chicken stock

Canned sliced mushrooms

1 pound chicken livers

Golden mushroom soup

DIRECTIONS:

In a medium bowl, mix salt, flour and pepper. Place livers into this mixture and toss to cover. Cook bacon on a skillet, over the medium heat). Remove and drain with paper towels.

Place the livers into the same skillet and cook until lightly browned. Place the livers and bacon into Slow Cooker. Pour in the chicken stock. Add golden mushroom soup and wine.

Cook under the lid for 6 hours. Use LOW temperature mode.

**Nutrition: Calories: 352 Fat: 16g Carbohydrates: 21g
Protein: 24g**

Slow Cooker Chicken with Italian dressing

This melts in the mouth!

Prep time: 19 minutes Cooking time: 6 hours Servings: 7

INGREDIENTS:

Sea salt

1 pack angel hair pasta

Pepper

Malt vinegar

1 tsp garlic powder

Ground cumin

Plain flour

Italian seasoning

Sour cream

Italian salad dressing

Parmesan cheese

DIRECTIONS:

In a bowl, whisk pepper, garlic powder, paprika, salt, cumin, cumin and Italian seasoning. Add Italian dressing, Parmesan, cream of mushroom soup, vinegar, flour, sour cream.

Set Slow Cooker to low. Cook for 6 hours using LOW temperature mode. Shred the chicken, continue cooking.

Separately, cook angel hair.

Serve chicken over the cooked pasta.

Nutrition: Calories: 483 Fat: 25g Carbohydrates: 40g Protein: 24g

We have actually come to the end of this wonderful as well as abundant Dishware Pot pressure cooker.

Did you get a kick out of trying these brand-new as well as tasty dishes?

We absolutely want so, along with a lot more will certainly turn up promptly.

To highlight the restorations, always incorporated with our delicious as well as likewise healthy and balanced as well as well balanced recipes of physical activity, this is a pointers that we mean to offer due to the fact that we consider it one of the most efficient mix.

A huge hug as well as we will be back quickly to maintain you business with our meals. See you rapidly.